Painting on Glass

Didier Carpentier   Joël Bachelet

ARCO PUBLISHING, INC.
215 Park Avenue South, New York, NY 10003

Published 1984 by Arco Publishing, Inc.
215 Park Avenue South, New York, NY 10003

Originally published in France under the title
Peinture sur verre
Copyright © 1980 Dessain et Tolra

Design and photography by the authors

Translated by M. S. Rohan

English edition copyright © 1982 EP Publishing Limited

Printed in Belgium by Offset Printing Van den Bossche.

Library of Congress Cataloging in Publication Data

Carpentier, Didier.
  Painting on glass.

  Translation of: Peinture sur verre.
  1. Glass painting and staining. I. Bachelet, Joël.
II. Title.
TT298.C3713 1984 - 748.5'028'2 - 84-3021
ISBN 0-668-06237-1 (pbk.)

Contents

1
2

Introduction

It may be true that the severe discipline and hard apprenticeship of the traditional art of painting on glass has left it, like so many other once-popular art-forms, in the hands of a privileged few. But that is no reason for it to stay shut off from a wider public. Glass painting has suffered for too long from being thought of as a sophisticated and yet somehow less than serious art, the semi-magical province of a few great masters. Rich as the field is, therefore, a great majority of artists and craftsmen tend, rather arbitrarily, to neglect it, and to us it seemed both useful and opportune to show that there are other ways of tackling it. The development of whole new ranges of synthetic paint—varnishes, colourants, resins and many others—have opened up fresh and exciting possibilities for the art of light and highlight to which this book is devoted. We have set out to make it as easy as possible an introduction to these new techniques for readers who, like our ancestors, are deeply fascinated by the beauties of glass.

Glass-painting? Or stained-glass? The two techniques have gone hand in hand, often to the point of being combined, in a centuries-old tradition of religious art. The grisaille, or grey-black shading, used on 15th century stained-glass is certainly one of the oldest forms of painting on glass. It suggested sculpted forms not unrelated to the architecture in which the windows were set. This heat-fixed painting was very like the painting we know today in its techniques, notably in demanding single brush-strokes which could not be retouched. In the centuries that followed, a more complex ornamental form of grisaille was developed for stained-glass, with the emphasis on the delineation and structuring of individual areas. The use of enamels began when glass-painting and stained-glass ceased to be purely religious and were used to decorate the great mansions of the Renaissance with subjects that might be heraldic or domestic or even from pagan mythology. The 18th century saw glass-painting become still more distinct from stained glass, as the first popular paintings on glass appeared. Between 1900 and 1914 the rise of Modern Style (essentially *Jugendstil* or *Art Nouveau*) encouraged the so-called *École de Nancy* to develop an essentially decorative style whose motifs and symbolism, inspired by Nature, draw from it a great pictorial lyricism.

This can be rediscovered in the many products of that period, but the things we paint will not need to be collector's pieces for them to take on, in our eyes, fresh associations and a whole new light.

Few of us have not got at least one old vase cluttering up our houses, or a period lamp, or just an odd assortment of bottles. Something very simple, even an old trademark picked out in colour, can give these unhallowed old relics a new lease of life and even make them into startlingly attractive *objets d'art*. Bottles, jars, glass boxes, glass crockery, glass-fronted cabinets, windows, table-tops, lampshades, glass jewellery, mirrors, sculpture, trays, fish-tanks and so on—it is an odd household that does not have something of the sort lying around, or that is not constantly using things in glass containers (perfumes, jams and jellies, liquor, medicines, chemicals, bath-essences, kitchen products and many more).

Easy, functional, flexible painting, on an everyday scale and easy to live with—that is what this book will be all about. In addition to a great deal of instruction and practical tips, the aspiring painter will also find a wide selection of different styles and themes to work on; we hope that the combined effect of these will be to awaken your own creative spirit and graphic sense. You will not need any tremendous artistic skills to handle any of the projects we have prepared for you. Simple procedures will help you to complete the design you choose, be it scraping, engraving, mirror-work, translucent glass or something three-dimensional, and perhaps even to adapt it to suit your own ideas. You will need only a few basic techniques to be able to create a design on the two main types of form:

1. Bottles, and similar containers generally without flat surfaces and impossible to paint on the inside.
2. Flat panes of glass, which can be worked on from the back as well as from the front.

We hope that all this interests you enough to let us be your first guides through this little-known but fascinating art form. And, if enthusiasm can really be infectious, we hope you will find ours properly contagious.

3

1. Monochrome stained-glass. 2. Modern etched-glass adaptation of a 17th-century icon. 3. Blazon painted in 'stained-glass' colours. 4. Sandblasted mirror decoration.

4

Tools and materials

Paints are the chief items you will need for working with glass. There are many kinds, designed for a wide variety of processes. You should do your best, therefore, to choose the most appropriate kinds for each of them. On the other hand, a smallish choice of brushes will be enough for a great many projects. Brushes will generally last quite well, provided you remember to take a little trouble to look after them. Have a good supply of rags to hand, as well as solvents, cleaners and thinners appropriate to the paints you are using (such as alcohol, acetone, petrol and so on). It will be difficult to make a good job of glass painting without these around you. You should therefore provide yourself with enough painting materials to handle both your first practice pieces and your final compositions. Use glass from about 3 to 5mm thick. You should also have the usual drawing implements to hand, and carbon paper to transfer your designs. For some designs a very sharp craft-knife and some well-tempered razor blades will be useful, and some dilute hydrochloric acid.

Transparent paints

These are sold as 'stained-glass' paints. They are actually coloured varnishes, which only become stable once dry, unlike model paints. No superimposition is possible, therefore. They can be used straight, slightly thinned with an equivalent colourless varnish or heavily diluted with an appropriate solvent (turps or white spirit). Mixing of colours from the same range is usually no problem, so you will not necessarily need to buy every colour in the range. It is not advisable, though, to try blending different makes of paints.

Cold ceramic paints

The same general points apply to these ranges of paints, which when dry have the look of kiln-fired vitrified glaze colours. Like the transparent paints, they are applied by brush, but to make them opaque an undercoat is usually needed. Colours can be superimposed once they have dried for an hour. These paints will not stand high temperatures, and should *never* come into contact with foodstuffs.

Model paints

These are excellent for large areas, and designs that have to be completely opaque. They are absolutely stable, and can be applied straight or mixed with others from the same range. Drying time varies from two to eight hours. They can, though, be superimposed after only 10 or 20 minutes, depending on how soft they are.

Gouaches and acrylic paints

These are excellent for monochrome designs. Their great elasticity makes them easy to apply. They can, in addition, be superimposed, and mixed among themselves before drying, and they are indelible. They do, however, have to be put on in very thin layers to prevent crackling.

Tube-applied paints

These are applied with the special nozzles on their tubes, so that they stand out as raised lines of different thicknesses. They are sold under trade-names such as *Cerncouleur* and *Color Magic*.

Bottle painting and under-glass designs

Bottles and the like are probably among the things most suited for glass painting, but whether it is transparent or opaque, it will always have to be on the exterior, since the limited access means that only a rare genius can get at the inside! The chiefest difficulty lies in getting the pattern for a design onto the surface to be decorated, whether this is cylindrical or otherwise curved. Because of this our first example is this little group of perfume bottles, painted, as will be all the pieces in the first part of this chapter, with transparent or 'stained-glass' paints.

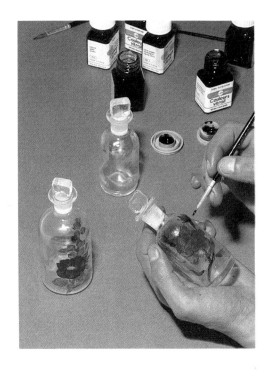

Transparent paints

Perfume bottles

It is hard to think of a fresher and more appropriate design than these three floral motifs—but the secret is in their spontaneity. In fact, all three are painted on directly, without guidelines. You need not feel obliged, therefore, to follow our version line for line (shifting a flower to right or left, for example). This method will give great flow and pliancy to the lines. Before beginning to paint the perfume bottles, you should clean them out carefully both inside and on the surfaces to be painted. Use 'stained-glass' colours.

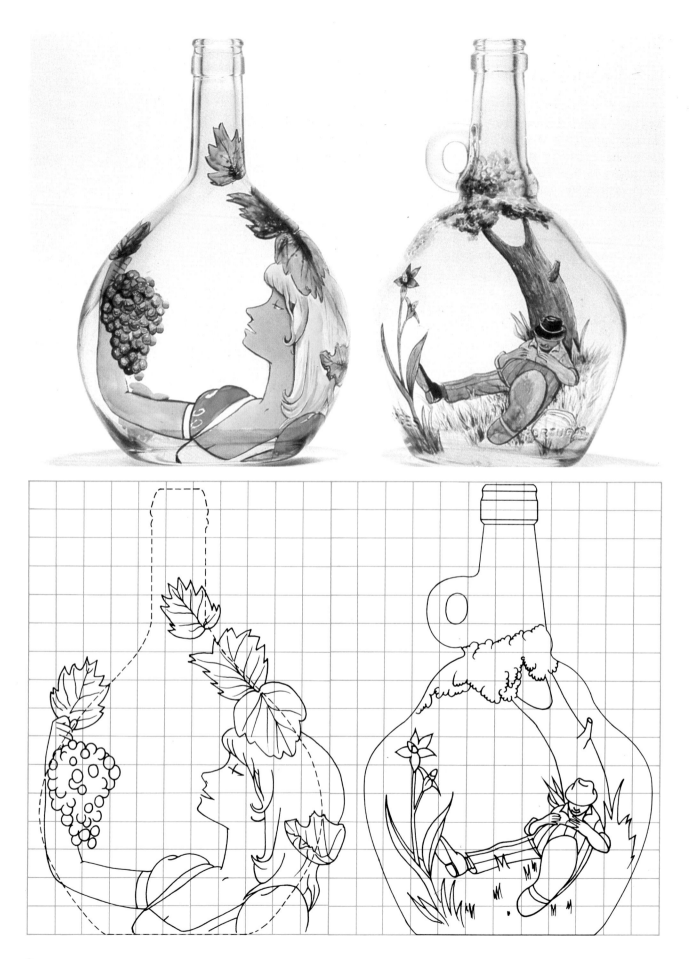

Spirit flasks

These two types of flask are common enough shapes, so you should not have too much trouble finding them. Faced with this kind of bottle, the first concern of someone who likes original designs should be to match theirs to the bottle, because the shape plays a primary role in making a unified composition out of the two elements, and solid and the graphic. An unmatched design is likely to end up a sorry mess. You absolutely must link the guidelines of your pattern to the lines of the bottle's own shape. In the first example, for example, that is why the line of the arm begins at the hand holding the grape and continues along it up to the neck, the hair and the leaves, also linking the angle of the left shoulder and the tips of the two lower leaves. Beyond these considerations, you can adapt the designs to suit yourself.

Clean the surfaces of the bottle with alcohol and transfer the design, using carbon paper, with as much flexibility as possible; you can enlarge or shrink the basic pattern using the squares. You do this by drawing larger or smaller squares and filling in, square by square, the lines of the original pattern.

When putting in the colour, go from the lightest to the deepest shades, laying down the paint in the visual 'rhythm', or direction, of the area you are painting. For uniform surfaces (the girl's arm, face and breast, picked out and highlighted in brown, yellow and red) use a wash, with paint well diluted with white spirit, laying the bottle flat to prevent drips and runs. Brushstrokes should be smooth and rapid. You will go over the edges, so do not forget to trim them off before the paint dries, using a brush dipped in thinner. Be careful to use a brush that will not shed bristles, and make sure that impurities will not get into either paint or thinner. No paint of the kind you are using will stand heavy superimposition. Every brushstroke should be clear and unique in itself, after a second or two to draw it out. Details and shading are added last (when each area is dry) with an opaque near-black, touch by touch. You can only make corrections with the craft-knife, never a brush; this would jeopardise the unity of line and the solidity of the design.

Oil lamp

A curious thing is this jellyfish-like oil lamp, apparently the product of one of the wilder outgrowths of the Art Nouveau movement. However, no drawn design need come between your creative fire and the form that inspires it.

This design shows us what a part painting by instinct and personal inspiration can play in glass work, and how fulfilling it can be even in such simple efforts.

Whisky service

The pattern here is linked to the purpose of the objects. Every piece bears the heraldic crest of Scotland, from whence its precious contents come. Work the same way for bottle and glasses. Thoroughly degrease the surfaces to be decorated with alcohol (methylated spirits), and trace the design onto fine tracing paper; it will be better if you do not transfer it directly with the

Adding medium tints after the lightest one

The frill on this oil lamp was painted with cold ceramic colours

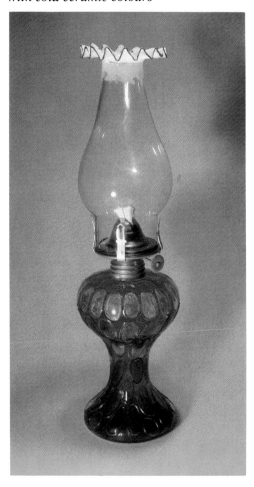

9

Painting the wild flower on a light-table

carbon paper, but use an alcohol-soaked cotton swab to wipe the back of the carbon and transfer the ink onto the reverse of the tracing. Stick this down onto the piece with sellotape and go over the tracing with a fine dry nib or ballpoint. These last precautions apply to every design whose density of lines makes using a transfer unavoidable. To clarify your design, lay the bottle on a white background and go over the lines with a rapidograph pen (02 for fine lines and 05 for thinner ones). Let this dry, then fill in the various areas with 'stained-glass' paint, avoiding going over the line. The bands appearing as white are added after the coloured areas they appear in are dry. The paint is scraped away gently so that the colourless transparency of the glass appears through. As a finishing touch, wait until the design is completely dry (two or three hours) and then apply transparent varnish from the same range over the whole design.

Opaque paints

Decorative plates

With these two patterns we make the transition from transparent to opaque paints, the one taking advantage of the transparency of the glass and the other reflecting the light back directly. But in these two designs the painting is done *underneath* the glass, which is to say behind the exposed surface of the piece, unlike the bottles. That lets you keep the upper side beautifully smooth.

The wild flower is done with the same transparent colours, however; what makes it different from the earlier pieces is that the appearance of the colours is accentuated by the opaque background to the design. There are two ways of achieving this effect: the plate can either be hung against a white or light-coloured wall—in which case the flower stands out more or less by itself—or add on a white or nearly white backing, which could be lacquer, paper or anything of that kind. In the first case you must be sure that the pattern reproduced and the projected picture are centred on the same optical plane, or almost. In the second case the picture will stand out clearly. The colours used must therefore be twice as light as you want the end result to look because they will intensify after they are put on. Begin painting with the lightest shades, and finish with the black shadings. Nuanced tones can be added to each area with blends of the appropriate colours.

The Farm-girl is very easy to manage. Transfer all the dark lines first, then when those are dry fill the colours in. Use reasonably thick model paints for that.

Farm-girl (Design in progress)

Two stages in the decoration of the swan's-neck using cold ceramic paints, stained-glass colours and opaque matt paint

Swan's-neck

This attractive bottle is also a recycled product. Its shape already suggests the sweeping rhythm of the final design. The work consists only of decorating the surfaces defined by the contours of the bottle's surface. This greatly simplifies the design, because when you are planning the piece all you have to do is let yourself be guided by the lines you see; give your imagination and colour sense the green light and try to translate what the piece suggests to you into painted form without using a preliminary design. For this particular bottle three kinds of paint were used—'stained-glass' colours for yellow and red ochre, glossy cold ceramic colours for the blue and white, and matt plastic covering paint for the black.

Before painting always remember to clean the surfaces to be painted well. Choose glass that is only lightly tinted—or, better still, colourless. That way you will have no trouble trying to fit it into your chosen colour scheme. Heavily coloured glass you will have to allow for if you are not looking for a nasty surprise; on blue glass transparent yellow becomes green and red goes dark chestnut. Start off with the 'stained-glass' paints you are using, because these will not go on over opaque colours, which can cause trouble at margins. Lay down the base colours first, and add the touches on top later. Next, follow the same rules with the blue and white cold ceramic colours, not forgetting to first put on an undercoat to ensure their stability and opacity. Apply the black last of all, only over absolutely dry paint.

Preserve jars

There is no reason to be afraid of humour in decoration, any more than of experiments in developing a really useful household sign-language, reflecting the need to rationalize the product—consumer relationship. Our symbolic figures here embody the images that some everyday foodstuffs summon up in the consumer's mind—'Now where on earth are those gherkins?' The object and its practical visual symbolism will establish the necessary dialogue—'Hi! Over here, I'm Mr. Gherkin, nice to see you! I'm just up here on the shelf in front of you, right between Ms. Tomato and Mr. Sweetcorn!' Life is full of little surprises, however, and when you take the jar down you find it contains mixed pickles.

For a number of fairly obvious reasons these designs are painted on the outside. Firstly, it is hard to get enough freedom of movement even in a wide-necked jar to paint the inside. Secondly, you dare not let the paints come into contact with foodstuffs. However, the jar exteriors can be cleaned off easily enough, with a damp sponge.

To begin with, degrease the surface carefully and transfer the pattern, enlarged by squares as before, using carbon paper. Paint on the main colours, one after the other from different palettes. We cannot give you any idea of proportions for blending because these depend on the choices of shade and intensity in the particular make you are using. It is not really important which colour value goes on first; what matters is the size of the areas to be

covered. Do the largest areas first, then the smaller ones. If these latter areas are superimposed (the eyes and the teeth of the gherkin, for example) wait till the underneath layers are completely dry. Finish with the lines and shadings (black and white), in the opposite order to the *Farm-girl*.

1

Wine bottle

Opaque paints cannot have subtle shadings or gradations of colours. On the other hand, you can manage these with lines, as is demonstrated by this suitably sober motif on a wine bottle, recalling its happy origins. The gently tapering waisted shape complicates transferring a pattern, because flat sheets of paper cannot be correspondingly distorted. Putting a design onto the curved surface becomes a difficult business, therefore, and it will be best to paint it directly onto the bottle, after you have carried out the usual procedures of degreasing the area to be painted and laying down a suitable undercoat before using the cold ceramic colours.

The second stage, as in the previous design, consists of filling in the areas of solid colour, the barrel being the largest. Check that the paint is at least touch-dry, even if slightly sticky, and only then add the visible elements of the design, the details and the shading on top. You should wait twenty minutes or so before trying this, by which time the paint should be stable enough not to come off on your fingers or leave messy prints. You can trim off the edges by scraping the dry paint away with the craft-knife.

1. Putting the finishing touches on the wine bottle. 2 and 3. Decorating a vodka bottle using a stencil. (Design in progress)

Vodka bottle

The interesting thing about this design is the way it is put on—by stencil, an outline cut out of a mask placed over the area to be decorated, and filled in with paint. The masking material is self-adhesive film, onto which you transfer the design (which is a suitably imperialistic doubleheaded eagle, in the best heraldic traditions) and then cut cleanly round it.

Be careful: you must apply the film with the greatest care. If it is not completely stuck down there is a risk that paint will run under its edges; for that reason also, use fairly thick model paint and a largish brush. The four colours are not superimposed, only juxtaposed as they are filled in. The next step is to scrape out the various lines, having painted in the crowns and the eyes once the film has been removed.

2

1. The Pitcher People (Design in progress). 2. Spring, a jug decorated by the same technique, except that the area covered with flowers rests directly on the glass. 3. Laying down the large areas of colour on the first two pitchers

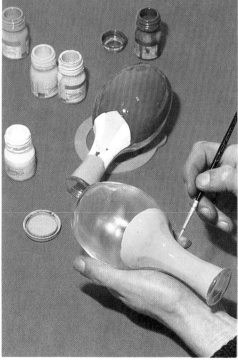

Pitcher people

May I introduce Monsieur and Madame Bon-Viveur, a charming little pair of wine jugs who are determined to have you share their inexhaustible *joie de vivre*—and also *manger* and, especially, *boire*—of which you may be sure they are past masters.

You will have little trouble finding two pitchers of the right shape, which several manufacturers are now producing. On the other hand, you will have a terrible time putting on the pattern by tracing or carbon paper, for the same reason as on the last piece—but here the bulges are even worse. The best method, therefore, is to paint it on directly, using reference points located by measurement. Use cold ceramic paints. Prepare enough paint to give each colour area two coats (remembering to leave ample drying time in between). Finish off with the details, adding them onto the coloured areas. Retouching is easy enough in this process, provided, here again, that you are careful of the drying time.

Filling in sandblasted areas

Decorated bottles

Strange old soda-water bottles of all shapes and dates, like these, still turn up sometimes in attics and junk-shops. Most of them have some sort of trademark or inscription, ground into the glass by sandblasting. It will be this inscription, and the often quite elaborate motifs that often accompany it, that we will be trying to bring out with paint. The point of the exercise, though, is not so much to get experience of letter design as to gain an understanding of the manner and style of retrospective decoration.

For this type of operation almost any indelible paints will do, as long as they are opaque and glossy. Because of the excellent definition of the designs, you will not need to use many colours on soda-water bottles. Plain single-colour paintwork, backed up if need be by one or two complementary shades, will be enough to bring out the inscriptions. You must remember to follow all the same preparatory directions as for the previous pieces (interior cleaning, degreasing). Use a medium-sized brush (no. 3 or 4) and trim off any surplus paint over the edges with a craft-knife.

16

Added extras

Other elements and decorative principles can be incorporated into glass painting. The following group of pieces can therefore call on—in addition to opaque and transparent paints—coloured cabochons (round-topped costume jewels), black *Cerncouleur*, sparkling or metal-flake paints, rub-on transfer letters and adhesive films.

Decorating the gooseberry jelly jar. The lines of the white area are produced with the craft-knife

Jampots

Begin by painting any areas you are going to *before* you begin adding the outside elements in your designs. Then fix the cabochons to their chosen places with glass adhesive. You will not need a transferred pattern; the suggested designs can be varied as much as you like, provided that your cabochons, as fruit, coincide naturally with the rest of the vegetable matter. The glue used sets at once, so do not dither about fixing the cabochons because you will find it difficult to get them off again. Then apply the black *Cerncouleur* to form the stalks, and the outlines of leaves and fruit. Hold the *Cerncouleur* tube like a pen; place its nozzle against the surface and apply a light pressure to squeeze it out into the desired line. Do the same for the inscriptions, 'Mirabelles' (plums) and 'Cerises' (cherries). Then fill in the leaves with the sparkling *Color Magic*, which comes in the same form as the *Cerncouleur*. To finish, rub on the transfer letters for 'Confiture' (jam or preserves) and 'Myrtilles' (bilberries), just as on the next piece.

Eau de cologne bottles

When the question of 'That's yours!' and 'That's mine!' arises, you may urgently need some way of distinguishing the two. For example, a woman's cologne really does little more for a man than the average male cologne does for a woman—however little the result would shock people these days. But no matter how you feel about that, it is still a good thing to know which is your own bottle. And since it is *eau de cologne*, why not leave the inscriptions in French—'Toi' and 'Moi' look a lot neater and more chic than 'You' and 'Me'!

It is nice to have the two words the same colour, but they need not be done the same way. Here, 'Toi' is made up of self-adhesive transfer letters, such as Letraset, sold as alphabetical sheets. They are best put on with an applicator, a kind of stiff rounded spatula that can press the letter smoothly onto the glass. The border is put on the same way. But be careful; these transfer films are so fragile that you will have to fix them with a special transfer varnish. 'Moi' is cut out of a self-adhesive film with a craft-knife, then laid directly onto the glass.

Eau de cologne bottles decorated with varnished press-on letters and self-adhesive film

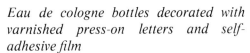

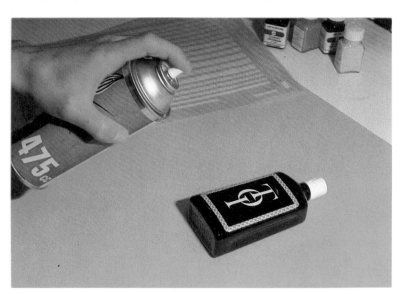

Single-colour painting on translucent glass

However tearful this sad clown is, you will not find it an unhappy job painting such an emotional, expressive and vibrant—but also very easy—subject.

On a lamp-globe, so that Pagliacci can radiate his sadness more effectively—that is where he has chosen to materialize, through the medium of a large brush well loaded with black. You will really be using the same technique as for transparent glass. The essential difference lies in the opacity of the paint, which must be absolute to stop the low-wattage bulb shining untidily through. For this you will have to put on several coats. Use very thick heat-resistant paint, therefore, and spread it out with a no. 8 brush to cover the larger areas. Work, if you can, with the shade in place and the light on, so as to catch any holes in the black area, and to homogenise the paint.

Be sure not to forget Pagliacci's single tear, sole outward sign of a blazing inner torment. Put that on with sparkling *Color Magic* paint (this range also includes green, black and gold). Then fold a suitable ruff out of thin card or cartridge paper.

Falling tear made with sparkling paint. (Design in progress)

Perfect example of the blending of two graphic techniques: use of line and of large bodies of colours in the monochrome scrape design on this sphere for a light-fitting. (Design in progress)

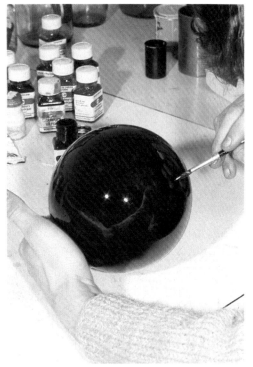

Scraping

This technique involves scraping away dry paint with a sharp object to reveal the base on which it was applied. The resulting design comes out in a kind of negative. The graphic elements (lines and solid areas) remain in the lightest part of the design, the colour of the glass beneath. The 'sharp object' is the craft-knife, which so far you have chiefly used for corrections, or a scraper-knife. Here the technique is reversed; corrections will be made with a brush. Despite the very spontaneous nature of the drawings, nobody is proof against slips and miscalculations. So, retouching has its uses. When scraping you will not need to press heavily on the glass; firstly, you might scratch it, and secondly, it increases your chances of skidding all over the place. Hold the knife like a pen, between thumb and index finger, perpendicular to the scraping motion. For wide cutouts you should lightly incise the paint, holding the cutter vertical. This will guide your scraping and give the cutout a clean edge. From time to time dust off the removed material which still clings by static electricity. Use a completely clean and dry no. 8 brush. For finer details use a scraping instrument with a really sharp point: a needle stuck into an old brush ferrule would be ideal.

Monochrome scraping

You do this with only one colour, and the result is unusually meant to be seen only as a transparency or on translucent glass. That is why you should use a dark, deep, wholly opaque paint, black or near-black. The series suggestions in this chapter are mostly wall-hanging plates, designed to let light through the design only. They provide some interesting examples of the variety of graphic effects you can manage simply with scraping.

Multicoloured scraping. 1. Filling in the areas of colour. 2. Marking in the lines with a craft-knife

1

2

In the landscape the plant life was depicted in a succession of strokes differentiated by their height (for distance), by their rhythm (for the general outline of the tree or plant) by their form (for the distinctive foliage of each of these) and by their intensity (for the depth of the design). The brightness of the ribbons is achieved by making the strokes parallel to the sides of each shape, gradually diminishing their intensity over the darkest areas, generally at right angles to the sides. The highlights on the fireworks picture were made by throwing out radiating lines from the centre of the airburst, and tipping some of these with little star motifs to suggest secondary bursts.

As the picture of the young lady and the duck illustrates, there is no need to cram a design with lines to bring out its essentials. A few judiciously-placed highlights will do more than enough.

Multi-coloured scraping

As its name suggests, this technique involves using several colours, generally chosen from the range of 'stained-glass' paints to ensure transparency and make the colour function as a filter between light and eye. It is readily used with a diffuser to let light through. You must first degrease the rear of the glass plate, and then paint it area by area. Next you must scrape away the lines which will show through as spectacularly white, much more difficult to manage sparingly because the paint flakes away (very inadvisable, in any case, for getting a smooth surface with some colours).

Carry out your scraping the same way as before, turning the plate upside down on a sheet of white paper so that the lines stand out better.

Glass panels

This chapter will deal with the main aspects of decorating flat glass, and especially 'live', that is, without physical or chemical transformation of the glass.

The approach to the design used has the advantage of being more straightforward than with bottle-painting. So is the actual execution of it. In effect, the design is transferred automatically without carbon paper or anything else, because, unlike a bottle, a flat sheet of glass can simply be laid down flat on the design—which is why this must be a tracing, so that when you turn the glass over the decoration behind will appear the right way round. How you paint the glass depends on the form of decoration you aim for—on transparent glass, opaque, translucent and so on. The paints will remain the same as for bottles and plates; it is what you do with them that will change.

Blazon

A heraldic shield with a mighty past behind it, that of the French city of Arras. (You could also use the Scottish crest provided for the whisky service—on p. 62.) Paint this pattern very carefully, keeping to the original colours.

Transferring the black outlines of the blazon directly with opaque paint

Colouring it in

23

Floral plaque

Flower motifs go with almost any style of drawing or painting without problem. The fluid textures of this floral plaque are yet another example of what can be done with the 'stained-glass' or coloured varnishes, used here with plenty of dash and vigour, which gives the panel a real vitality and a strange sense of movement.

Use transparent paints for this piece (see *Bottle-painting*), spreading the colours generously with bold strokes.

Frieze in white

The inspiration for this theme was cave art, rich with similar subjects shown 'flat', in only two dimensions, since our ancestors had not got the hang of perspective. On page 64 we give a sample of the kind of the kind of figurative elements suitable for this kind of decoration in white (plastic gouache). They are put on by self-adhesive film stencil, the same technique as used on the vodka bottle, only for this the stencils are saved and used repeatedly. Apply paint reasonably thickly on an impeccably cleaned and degreased surface, having first made sure that the stencil is positioned absolutely correctly.

1

3

1 and 2. Floral plaque. 3. Frieze in white

2

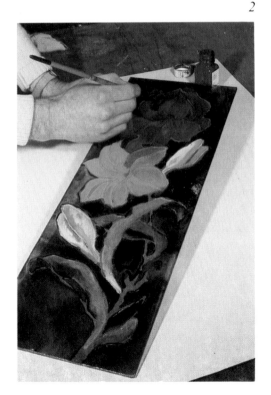

Flower garland, painted with model enamel and 'stained-glass' paints. (Design in progress)

Garland

The garland was originally a spiritual symbol, and even as a simple circlet of flowers it still keeps a kind of added beauty. A certain secret splendour, rich and eternally renewed, seems to cling to it. The rich base element of our design is taken from a style well adapted to coping with the problems of repeated concentric motifs. It is used eight times, around a circle made with compasses. The first thing to do, therefore, is to trace the two flowers of the composition, the open and the closed orchid, which together make up a sector (a subdivision of a circle, between two radiuses), and transfer them, at the desired size, eight times around the drawn circle.

This done, lay the pane of glass on the drawing, having first cleaned it off very carefully on both sides. Transferring the black outline is done automatically be reproducing the design on the glass with black *Cerncouleur* or brush. If you prefer to use the brush, you will find it most convenient to use unthinned model paint. Move the pane clockwise over the tracing as you work, anticlockwise if you are left-handed. This is because the paint will not dry instantly, and you otherwise risk smearing it with your arm. The brush will let you reproduce the various thicknesses of line, and so preserve the subtlety of the design.

The painting must be done carefully. Use 'stained-glass' paint for this, and apply it as uniformly as you can, so that the brush strokes do not show. Put on the violet first, and see how intense the green should be in relation to it.

Lines in Cerncouleur

Corner lamps

The goodness of a hot summer's day, the delicate fluttering of a butterfly, the wide-eyed joy of a child, the loving kiss of clear water, the tenderness of a mother, the cosiness of a kitchen and the warmth of bedtime.... We shall delight, rather in the Carl Larsson manner, in those moments of great happiness that a softly glowing light will reawaken not only in a corner of our room but of our hearts.

These four great moments of the day—bathtime, walking, suppertime and bedtime—each form a part of a pair of rectangular corner lamps which we will be showing you how to make. Each one is made up of four pieces of glass, two of them painted (the visible faces) and two of smoked glass (those in the angle of the corner). The glass panes used should measure 500 × 250mm. First, using the squares method, enlarge the first design to the size you want on a tracing, so as to reverse the subject, which should be painted on the outer side of the glass (although seen as a transparency). Then fix the tracing on a white sheet of paper and place the glass over it.

Unlike our previous efforts using 'stained-glass' paints, as these lamps will, no black lines will be used to mark the areas of colour. The colours here will have to be put on directly, without the help of a guideline. This will be the main difficulty in painting these four designs. As we have seen, nuances of colour cannot be transferred, except in certain very precise cases; hence the need to put on the paint directly. The second awkwardness lies in the way colours will vary in intensity between the image as it is painted over the design and as it will appear in transparency once the lamp is assembled and in use. The process is exactly the opposite of what we saw happen in the case of the rose on the plate, the image faint when painted intensifying once it is on the wall. It is important to take account of this optical phenomenon and paint with colours twice as intense as usual if you do not want to end up with an image two times paler in the light.

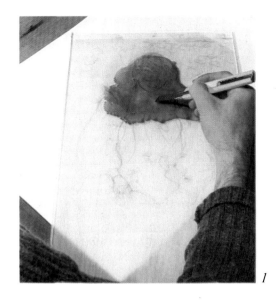

1

The success of this kind of design (the bathtime, the walk) also depends on other factors, essentially pictorial. 'Stained-glass' paints even out badly. So, to get a properly uniform surface (on the skin of your characters, for example) you must:

—be able to work on an absolutely level surface

—check that your brushes are not shedding hair, and that both paint and thinner are free from impurities

—measure out very precisely the proportions of paint and, most important, of thinner making up your colours.

After that, take a brush and cover the whole area to be covered with paint, going widely over the margins. In spreading itself out the very liquid paint will become even. Guide it by taking the pane in both hands and lifting it lightly in all directions. When the paint is evenly spread lay it down again. All these operations should be done quickly. Then, with a metallic point (blade or scraper nib) shade down the colour to get tone variations. This you do by pushing aside the still liquid paint with the tip of the point to make a lighter shade of the same colour appear in that area. Before the paint dries, clean round the margins of the colour area with a cloth, then when the paint is dry trim the edges with a craft-knife. You can then scratch lightly at the paint to accentuate lighter areas and begin to add details with the brush: eyes, mouth, nose, and so on. Handle faces and exposed body areas this way. Then paint the hair (with rapid free strokes, using almost pure tone), the clothes, from lightest to deepest (for the little girl's dress, shade first and add the checkered pattern afterwards) and finish off with the fine details. As a rule, 'overlapping' details are added after the base they go over (such as the grass and the hat over the dress, and the poppies on the grass and the dress).

2

You will in fact have to scrape away their exact outlines before adding their respective colours, because 'stained-glass' paints cannot be superimposed. Outline the pitcher, piece by piece, by scraping away the things 'behind' it. Refine the highlights of the white negligée with the knife, as also the water splashing over the little girl. Put on the other parts of the design now, and finish off with the background colours. For those of the bath scene you will have to trace off the exact outlines of the areas to be left unpainted. Cut this out and stick it on a slightly smaller tracing-paper cut-out. The resulting combination must cover these same areas perfectly before you stencil around it with a brush. For this use a mixture of pure violet.

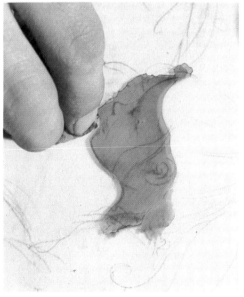

3

With these two panels complete, you only have to stick them together with aquarium glue and to put a lamp unit giving off a warm light inside, with some kind of light diffuser (tracing-paper, parchment, acetate film, and the like) before you begin making your second lamp, featuring *Suppertime* and *Bedtime*.

4

5

Corner lamp: 1. Tones added on the mother's face. 2. Putting on the body of colour which will become the child's face. 3. Trimming down the paint. 4. Scraping away spaces for foreground elements. 5. The Walk, on completion (shown full-on). 6. Pattern for Suppertime (full-on view). 7. Pattern for Bedtime, full-on. 8. Bathtime, detail of scraping. 9. Bathtime, full-on view. 10. Bathtime, laying down background shading over a protective stencil. 11. The lamp with its light lit inside

6

7

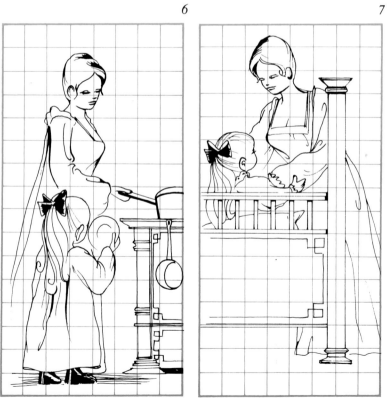

8

9

11

10

Little theatre on four levels

Introduced into Europe by Italian troupes, the *commedia dell'arte* is probably one of the most influential theatrical forms ever. The energy of the acting and the marvellous mime elements have kept its appeal even for modern audiences, and we cannot overestimate the influence it has had on the development of theatre. It was the ancestor of forms as far apart as the comedies of Molière in France and pantomime and Punch and Judy in Britain (look at the character on stage right; he is called Polichinello). This three-dimensional composition will recreate for us the performance of a troupe of *buffoni* in the 18th century, on an outdoor stage in the grounds of a great, possibly a royal, *chateau.* . . .

This decorative panel happens to be made up of four planes which together will form a kind of picture in 'relief'. Each plane is left partly transparent, painted on the back and set in the same line of sight, at right-angles to it with the panes equally separated. The difficulty of this kind of picture is therefore that of breaking down a picture into separate planes. If ordinary glass is used, four is the maximum number of panes usable in such a 3-D panel, because all glass sold as transparent and colourless simply is not—there is always a slight tint! For ample proof, look what happens when you pile up a few panes onto a sheet of white paper; as layer succeeds layer the coloration very quickly becomes apparent. We have made this design easier for you by giving you patterns for the four panes composing it. All you need do is enlarge them to the size you want (using the squares again—add your own this time!) and transfer them to the backs of your panes. Do this by placing the glass on the tracing, itself fixed to a sheet of white paper behind. If you want to develop your own design, be sure that the cutout (clear) areas of each piece match those of the next one closely, this for the top three planes (the fourth being the background, it should have no cutout).

Transfer each pattern onto each pane with a fine brush and black model paint. No need to worry if the lines overlap somewhat from one sheet to the next, they will not show up after you have filled the colours in (on the same side, using model paints). Paint close up to the lines, leaving no gaps, but do not go over; do not risk superimposing until the paint underneath is sufficiently dry.

Set the panels, once dry, in equidistant grooves in two wooden blocks (14mm deep by 7mm high).

Monitoring your painting by suspending the glass over a mirror

The finished piece assembled in its grooves

Outlines and colour-charts for the four perspective planes (A, B, C, D)

Fixing the paints with a protective coat of varnish

Siren

Don't trust her. This unusual mermaid can be as terrible as she is beautiful, because, even if her curvaceous elegance is rivalled only by the precision of her lines and the elegance of her colour-scheme, she has a poison hidden away in those spines that will cool off even the most ardent admirer. Even so, we have dared to make her the subject of this original aquatic composition, done in coloured varnishes ('stained-glass' paints). She will be as happy in an under-glass picture as on the glass of a suitably shaped aquarium.

She is painted in much the same way as the whisky service. But the pattern (page 63) is transferred directly by placing the pane (unlike other pane-paintings) onto a same-size tracing, itself backed with white paper. In the case of an aquarium the painting *must* be on the outside to avoid contact with the water, and to keep the brilliance of the gold. First go over the lines with pen or rapidograph, then paint it, then fix the result with aerosol varnish.

Putting on the Cerncouleur

Imitation stained-glass

Why not let the light of ancient stained-glass windows show us the turmoil of a knightly tournament, for example, or of a terrible fight to the death across which mighty antagonists face each other, blazons and harness aslant.

Let us also not forget that the honour of a lady frequently entered into the dispute, which explains the intensity of the colours we have chosen for this mock stained-glass window. Mock, because it is all one piece, but stained-glass, because we use 'stained-glass' colours on a surface subdivided very like the real thing, only more easily.

Begin, as usual, by enlarging the design with squares to the size you want. For this, make yourself a little grid on the same scale as

Putting on Color Magic

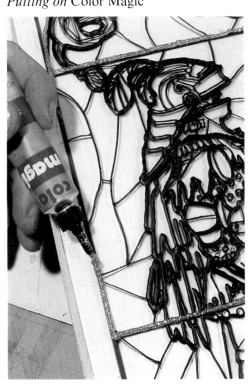

the photograph, and reproduce this on tracing paper in a larger scale, adding in the corresponding lines of the drawing. The essential thing is that every detail should be reproduced exactly. Then place a pane of glass (not too thick) over the tracing and reproduce the black lines on the glass with the aid of *Cerncouleur* tubes to simulate the look of leading, one for thick lines and one for thin. The design uses two thicknesses of line; for the main lines use a *Cerncouleur* tube with a wide nozzle, and for the subdivisions one with a narrower nozzle.

Painting should present no problems. All the same, take account of the characteristics of your paint. Shade your colours in the appropriate areas as you go along, and do not go back over them if you want to avoid leaving brushstrokes. Leave white areas bare; the colourless glass will create the effect. Follow the same precautions regarding mixing and diluting of colours as on the previous projects using 'stained-glass' colours.

Cut the opaque surround out of expanded polystyrene 17mm thick. Make the outline of the stone surround by poking in the surface of the polystyrene, then paint the rest of the surface black. Then position its openings carefully round the design and stick it down onto the glass.

Blotterfly

This extraordinary creature was spawned by an experiment—in folding, not genetics—in which chance seems to have been messing about somewhat with the usual anatomy of the *lepidoptera*. But however that may be, the result is rather more interesting as a study in textures and forms, using very elementary painting techniques. How the colours will arrange themselves on the paper is in the hands of chance.

Begin by providing yourself with a sheet of fairly thick paper; fold it along the centre and spread it out again in front of you. Then lay down streaks and blobs of water-based gouache on half the sheet only, following your whim and your general idea of how a giant butterfly should look. How you arrange and distribute the colours is entirely up to your imagination, provided you put down enough for them to blend without leaving gaps. Then fold the blank half over onto your half-butterfly outline, pressing the two sides together for a few moments. Then unfold it and transfer the sheet onto your pane of glass before the paint can begin to dry. Again, apply the design by rubbing the back lightly. But be careful: hold it firmly so it does not slither and smear the design. Finally, peel it off and let the result dry.

It is rare for every transfer to come out well, so you may have to do the whole thing over again.

When you think one of your species is worthy of survival, add some final touches of sparkling paint to elevate it to the level of high art. But before that, you could always add a couple of cabochons here and there. . . .

The blotterfly's life-cycle

Bouquet on gilt

The eyecatching effect of this pattern is achieved by a combination of cabochons, sparkling paints and gilt, with transparent paint playing only a very small part. The glittering look of the main materials is the basis of the design style

To begin making a bouquet of this kind, first work out on a piece of paper how you will arrange your cabochons to look like the flowers you choose. You should probably use at least two sizes of cabochon together for greater flexibility—asymmetrical flowers, concentric flowers, the choice is up to you. In any case, stick the cabochons on quickly with glass adhesive *after* you have cleaned the glass.

The second step is to paint on the stalks and leaves, following the lines of your pattern, with sparkling paint. You can go over the thicker lines several times if you want to. The sparkling paint is applied in much the same way as *Cerncouleur;* hold the *Color Magic* tube nose down, pressing the nozzle opening against the line to be covered, then move it along, squeezing the sparkling material lightly out. After this is dry, fill in the outlined surfaces of the leaves with whatever transparent colour you choose. Let all of this dry.

The last step is carried out on the other side of the glass, so you will need to be very sure it *is* dry before you turn it over. Get gilt powder from a paint dealer and dust it as evenly as possible over the surface you want to cover. Then fix it to the glass with spray varnish.

Putting on the cabochons

Making up the stalks

Cold-glazed tiles

All the look of something fire-glazed, without the expense of a kiln and equipment, a richly complex design without the difficulties of aleatory (random) technique, this is what a newly-developed process using synthetic resins and colourants can give us. It allows you to create a great range of colours and shades, from the most vibrant to the subtlest.

As always, the first thing to do is to clean off your glass pane. Buy yourself several colorants, some resin and some hardener (they are generally sold in craft or DIY shops). Provide yourself with some clean jars for the various mixing operations. The composition of the base should be one part hardener to two parts resin, thoroughly mixed together.

Mark out your surfaces with *Cerncouleur* or sparkling paint. If you want shaded tones, first pour out some of the base mixture onto the marked-off area and then add the colourants, mixing them in with a pin or matchstick. If you want solid tints, add the colourant into the base mixture before spreading it onto the surface. You have a choice of two kinds of colourant, opaque or transparent. You can use them together easily enough. Cold glaze is workable for an hour at about 20°C. It dries in three hours, but only hardens fully after 24 hours. If it hardens too quickly or too slowly, your proportions are wrong, and you should start again. Be careful: liquid resins can cause skin irritations and rashes. It is important to wash your hands thoroughly in alcohol or soap and water.

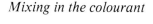

Mixing in the colourant

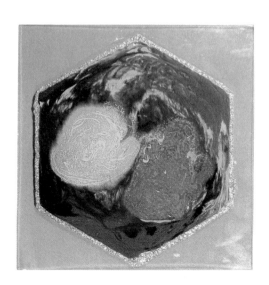

38

Mirrors

You may have wondered about how designs or inscriptions are put on mirrors—given the chiefest problem, the infuriating double image that even the least mark on the glass creates. But how to get to the silvering? How to get through the glass, the only way of avoiding that shapeless double image? How to keep the perfect surface we see from the front of the mirror? The moment you take away the silvering you completely destroy the reflective

Various stages in the creation of a mirror decoration produced by freehand scraping without a preliminary design. Here the designs are elaborated progressively as the protective backing is scraped away with a razor blade

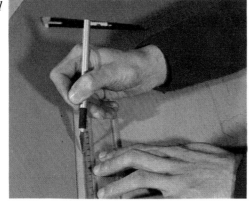

effect—a vicious circle. But there is a way of answering all our rhetorical questions. Together we are going to study a technique for preserving the parts of a mirror that you do not want to paint (which is what it amounts to). In the course of this you will have the chance to paint for yourself one of those airy fascinating ladies whose swirling curves the painter Mucha was so fond of depicting.

Young girl with orchid

The guarded look of this lass with the flame-coloured hair seems to discern the faintest quiverings of her fresh-plucked flower. To capture her in your mirror—behind the glass, that is—you need only follow these instructions. First enlarge the design to fit your mirror by the usual method, then turn the tracing round. Everything is now done from this side. Transfer the design to the back of the mirror, taking care to reverse the tracing. With a craft-knife cut very lightly into the protective coating, following the contour of the silhouette, and scrape away the inside of the area to be painted with a razor blade—preferably the single-edged type. To protect your fingers, use the blade in a holder or cover it with some Sellotape. This second step, remember, is to remove *only* the protective coating. Use the blade carefully, therefore, so as not to scratch the silvering—which is fiendishly difficult—and, most of all, not to scratch the glass. To do this, hold the blade between thumb, index and third finger, keeping it constantly flexed and aslant. Having scraped away the whole painting area, touch up anywhere you have gone over the margin or your blade has slipped with an engraving varnish, and let that dry. Straight lines are best done with a steel rule and a craft-knife.

6

40

The next step is the complete removal of the silvering, at normal temperature. You do this with hydrochloric acid at 10 to 20% dilution. Brush the acid and water solution onto the silvering, and then if you haven't already done so, go away and open a window! Do not breathe the fumes. Leave the acid to 'bite' for 4 to 8 minutes, longer if the acid has already been used. When the silvering has totally disappeared from the chosen spots rinse the mirror *thoroughly* under the tap. If any acid has splashed onto your skin or clothing, wash it off very thoroughly. Finally, wipe the mirror dry and begin putting on the colours (gloss model paint, used as for the theatre design).

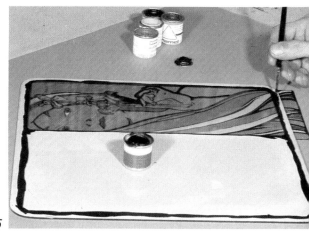

5

1. Cutting the frame. 2. Scraping away the protective backing. 3. Etching with acid. 4. The desilvered pane. 5. Painting the reverse of the pane. 6. The finished design

7

8

Behind the glass (7 and 8)
Nothing obliges you to paint the bared areas of your mirror; you can display photographs there, or any other document with decorative value or associations. This, a kind of island in the reflective surface, is a fascinating extension of technique for the mirror worker

The papers you choose should be flattened against the mirror when you are ready to put them on. Then shuffle them around once or twice to find which way of distributing them looks best. Superimpose any you would rather not cut

Street-urchin

This monochrome design is particularly interesting because its scraped-away areas are much finer and more detailed than the last pattern, and so harder to cut out. It demands tremendous precision, but is otherwise much the same in the execution. Painting it, on the other hand, is simpler because there is only one colour.

Transferring the urchin design and scraping it out. Fill the acid-cleared areas in with firm brushstrokes; behind the remaining silver go over the margins as much as you like. (Design in progress)

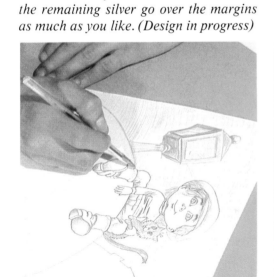

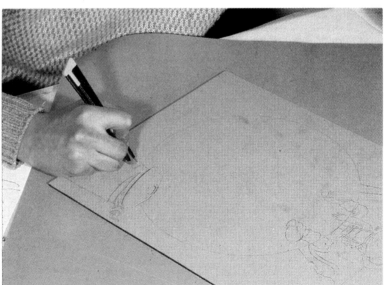

1

2

Four-seasons mirrors

We are sure you would enjoy painting one of our sumptuously personified Four Seasons, in a style inspired by Art Nouveau and Mucha in particular. Ethymical energy and fluid curves are happily united in a superior graphic design particularly well suited to mirror use. Their neat outline is easy to scrape out.

Over the page you will find photographs of Winter and Summer. We only give the pattern drawings for Spring and Autumn, but they are executed in just the same fashion—in what colours we leave to you. Each design includes a fairly narrow black frame, to be scraped out at the same time as the rest. For this, use a steel rule and cut the two edges of the band with a craft-knife. Then empty out the part between the two incisions, holding the knife like a pen and slicing outwards. That is the best way to minimize skidding. Cut the outlines of the ladies lightly, as in the first mirror pattern, so as to get a cleaner and crackle-free outline. You will find the same need for precision as when using the knife on 'stained-glass' colours (as with the corner lamps). Care in scraping this outline is important because it will mark the outer border of the painting, where it meets the mirror. It should be perfect.

Then, as for the orchid girl, dissolve off the silvering with dilute hydrochloric acid. Let it bite for the same time, and wash it off just as carefully. With the design showing through in clear light, begin painting with opaque model paints. Use gloss, for greater colour intensity. First copy the lines of the design with a no. 3 brush, then fill in the colours. Let the whole thing dry. All that the mirror will then need will be to have your dirty fingerprints removed.

4

1. Pattern for Spring
2. Pattern for Autumn
3. Winter. 4. Transferring the cutout
5. Desilvered pane
6. Winter (drawing in the black outlines)

Designs in progress

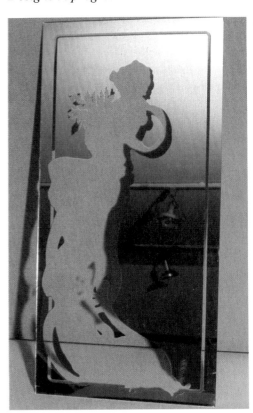

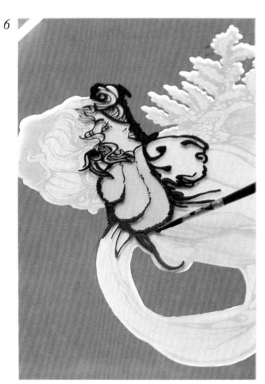

7. Summer (scratching away the protective backing). 8. Summer: it is impossible to get perfectly plane views of these mirror designs because of the difficulty of reflecting the camera, but enlarging them should be little trouble, because the distortion is only slight; only lateral parallax need be corrected)

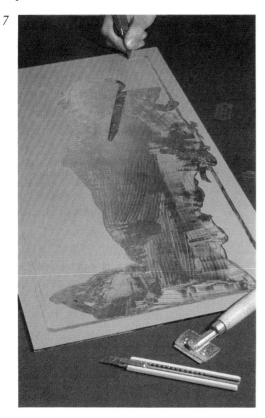

45

1. Applying the varnish. 2. Filling in the emptied areas with model paint

Stylized swan

He gazes out at us with so much resplendent grandeur, this mirrored swan, like the archetype of esoteric style.

The way this design is created differs from all the preceding ones by the way the area to be painted is cleared. This method can only be used on mirrors whose protective coating is soluble in thinner. More, it is recommended for very fragmentary designs because it is frequently easier to paint a small area than to scratch out its outline. That is exactly the case with this circular pattern, in which the feathers are made up of small intermediate areas that would be fiddling to scrape out.

Your first task is thus to take off the protective cover with the help of the right solvent, which will lay bare the silvering. Then clean off the whole surface with a preparation of vinegar and whiting. Wipe it off with damp cotton-wool. Then paint engraving varnish over all the areas where you will want the silvering to remain untouched by the acid, that is, the parts that are to remain mirror. Take care—lay on the varnish in a thick enough coat so the acid will not affect it. If not, you will have to halt the damage by adding an extra touch of black varnish. Apply the acid only after the varnish is wholly dry (about twelve hours) and in the same way as for the previous patterns.

To finish off, paint the prepared areas with opaque gloss paint, beginning with the black. Then recover the silvering with a layer of protective paint.

1 2

1. Painting in translucent enamels and grisaille. 2. Applying grisaille. 3. Combination of an enamelled pane with stained-glass elements. The linking of the two techniques, staining and enamelling, is very well exemplified here by this Orientally-inspired piece

3

Enamelled glass

The techniques we have developed up till now made use of paints and varnishes which coloured the glass as soon as they were applied. But there are other ways of painting glass. Colours can, in effect, be heat-set onto the glass. The process consists of bringing colourants made up of coloured crystals and metallic oxides to a temperature just below the melting point of glass (to around 650°C, in other words). We thought it might be interesting to introduce you in this chapter to this other form of glass painting which, like stained-glass, should be thought of not as complicated and obsolete, but as a completely different medium. It lets anyone who has an enamelling kiln, or access to one, try their hand at one of these original patterns especially suited to enamelled glass. Unlike under-glass designs, the enamels used on these decorative panels are translucent. Like stained-glass, they can be shaded in grisaille. This refers to the method of applying a half-tone of glass-paint (the 'matt') and then partially removing it, or modifying it, to produce a monochrome shading effect.

Enamelled glass is often useful for restoring old glasswork, and it can happen that one is asked to repair a deteriorated or broken design. You must then adopt the same techniques and the same colours (determined by tests) if you wish to create a perfect likeness to the original.

1

For this, clean both sides of the pane with vinegar and whiting mixture before going on to paint. Place the glass on a pattern enlarged to the right size, then, using a sable brush, mark in the lines with iron oxide paint mixed with gum arabic and thinned with dilute acetic acid or vinegar. Leave it to lie for at least a day in a dry atmosphere. Then add the shading and the grisaille with badger brushes. By now you should be practised enough to predict just how the general outline of the piece is going to look. Let the iron oxide dry again in the proper conditions. Then turn the piece over on white paper or on a light-table. Then, on the back of the piece, begin applying the translucent enamels, thinned with water, which will give the piece its colour after firing. Once the enamels are dry fire it once or twice as you prefer, side after side or both at once.

The two vertical compositions are done on the back of their glass, which is covered after firing with a uniform coat of black paint. They make no use of grisaille. The shadings are added at the same time as the colours. As a background the plate has a dappled texture made with black paint spread on with heavy brush strokes, through which superimposed gold paint can show. This very flexible method allows you to create shadings-down in large areas of colour.

1 and 2. Overpainted enamelled designs. 3. Composition in translucent enamels and grisaille

2

3

48

Etched glass

Etching introduces us to a new way of painting on glass, using relief designs as opposed to the work on smooth surfaces in our previous chapters.

In fact the unevennesses the etching process leaves in the glass are a perfectly valid means of decoration—because of the lively textures they create—to the extent that they are incorporated into the unity of the design. In any event, they must be so well tied in with the coloured elements of the composition that they look as planned as the painting.

Crystal glasses

Crystal objects are etched with a hydrofluoric acid solution. From the rather peculiar objects they once were, these glasses have become *objets d'art* of great richness. Their unaccustomed sparkle lends them that much-sought-after uniqueness, guaranteeing that they will never be mistaken for any other kind of glass.

Before anything else we must remember that strict precautions must be observed in handling the acid needed to etch the surface of the glass. The exact proportion of acid and dilutant (water) depends on the ambient temperature, the depth of etch required and the strength of the constituents. Hydrofluoric acid is extremely dangerous. It *must* be used *only* in a fume cupboard

with the extractor fan on—the fumes will attack the lungs if breathed in. The acid must be handled with extreme care, and full protective clothing must be worn, including rubber gloves, face mask and goggles.

Before applying the acid, protect all the areas not to be etched with a bitumen-based black varnish; this will oblige you to work out your design beforehand. Once the varnish is dry, don protective working gloves and bring the glass into contact with the acid. Control the state of etching constantly. Rinse the piece off with water several times if you need to, and stop when you are satisfied with the textures and relief you have obtained. You can etch by brushing the acid on, or by immersing the whole piece in it, provided that *all* the pieces to be protected (including the insides and the stems of your glasses) are covered with black varnish.

Strip off the varnish with a solvent, alcohol or petrol depending on the make. Then apply the paint to the reliefs, taking the same precautions as for the bottles. Use opaque gloss paint if possible.

Mother and child

How could one imagine that a mere painted plaque could convey so much love and tenderness so well? Even so, this admirable mother and child—executed with a wholly Italian sensibility and tenderness—are nevertheless painted on the back of a pane of glass etched out just like the crystal glasses. Preparing this kind of work demands a great deal of care. In such a case your first step is to prepare the design on a paper pattern. If you choose this composition, enlarge it with squares as usual. Then clean both sides of the glass and place it over the design. Then, applying the black varnish with a brush, protect all the areas of the front to be left intact, and the whole of the back and sides. Allow slightly larger areas, bearing in mind that the acid will reduce them slightly (the outlines of the flowers, that of the interior frame, and

1. Shield areas to be protected from etching with a black varnish. 2. Cleaning after etching and rinsing. 3. Laying down the first coat of gold. 4. Finishing touches on the scumbling. 5. Mother and child (plane view)

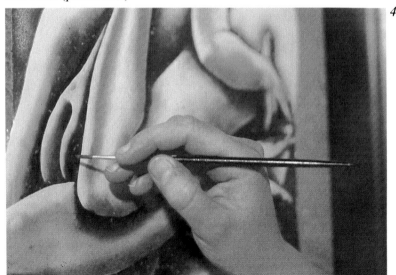

5

1

the whole of the figures). Let it dry for several hours before engraving the panel with a brush or by immersing it in an etching bath. Control the etching well. You must remain master of the situation at every step. For this reason you should refer back to the precautions set out under the section on crystal glasses; all these are of paramount importance. When the etching is finished rinse the glass thoroughly under the tap and strip off the black varnish with solvent.

Begin the painting by applying a first coat of opaque gold paint to the background (a base colour making it possible to gauge the other colours). Then add a first coat to opaque the figures, then a second the colour of the lightest skin tones. Then paint the outlines of the forms in the darkest colour of the design, and shade the colour by scumbling from those lines to create an effect at once very sharp and very subtly shaded. Use soft brushes, broad but not very thick. Do not forget the intermediate ochre shades, added the same way. Add in the details and the surrounding area of colour. Then to finish apply a last coat of gold on the background.

Icons

These sumptuous icons are made the same way. The main difference is their texture, because the whole surface is etched, except for the lines and the faces, which obviously means you will be painting over the engraved areas. The varnish for these can easily be put on by screen printing, which will make it possible to bulk-produce these pieces.

2

1. Screen for screenprinting on the protected lines of your design in black varnish. 2. Finished icon (plane view). 3. Piece in progress (filling in of facial areas)

3

The icons should be etched out with just as much care and precautions as before. The painting, though, is very fragmentary. It should be done area by area in the troughs of the etched areas so that the relief areas are free of it.

The faces having been kept smooth, they should be painted specially by the scumbling technique to keep the lines of the composition sharp, and with the same opaque colours. These icons being intended for wall decoration, their colours should completely blot out those of whatever ground they are laid against, but which should show through the transparent lines just surrounding the figures. The icon on page 4 has no transparency at all.

Sandblasting

Although, strictly speaking, this is a means of working the material rather than of decorating it, sandblasting can often be combined with glass-painting. In this chapter we will mostly be dealing with painting problems encountered after sandblasting, because this requires equipment that few amateurs could afford (1). We suggest you 'subcontract' the actual operation after you have prepared the masking yourself.

For this, begin by degreasing the glass. Apply a sturdy adhesive paper ('contact' or similar) to the rear of the pane. Transfer the design onto this, then incise the outlines of the areas to be exposed to the sand (2). These can as well be isolated areas as large separate surfaces on glass or on a mirror.

Then go and get the pane sandblasted, giving careful guidelines for the process, which uses corundum sand.

After this, remove the adhesive masking.

There are different ways of colouring a sandblasted pane, whether glass or mirror:

a. The patina left by gouache or coloured varnish ('stained-glass' paints). It often goes well with silver powder (11).

b. Metallic powder (gold, silver, bronze and the like) applied with a varnish.

The series of mirror tiles on these two pages was created by this process. Begin by degreasing the pane, then spread gilding varnish over the surface (3) and onto that fresh ground apply a layer at 20° of turpentine or white spirit. Note that the varnish can be tinted. Then spread on the gilt powder with a brush (4). Let it dry, then add the silver leaf, applying it with a finger. You can lightly oxidise the silver by interleaving the sheets with damp blotting paper; this gives them that marbled look. To finish, cover the whole thing with a coat of protective varnish or vinyl paint.

c. Aero paint is a kind of opaque gouache allowing you to elaborate light shades (13). The black results from a dark background reflected in the mirror area, a photographic difficulty you will notice in all the pictures in this section.

4

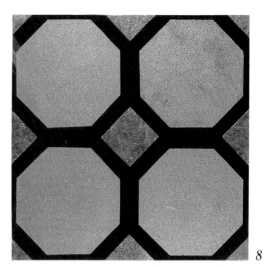

8

5

6

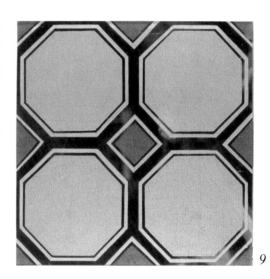

9

7

10

55

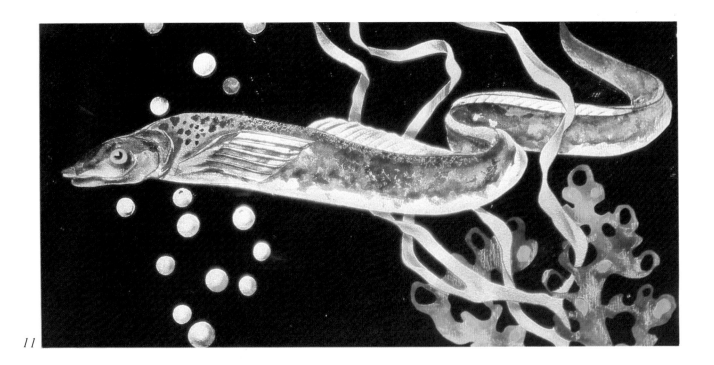

11

12

1. Sandblasting a piece. 2 to 8. Various stages in working on a mirror tile design. 9 and 10. Possible variants on the original design. 11. Mirror decorated with coloured varnishes and a silvery material. 12. Using an adhesive screen to protect areas to be left smooth. 13. Tile decorated in aero paint. 14. Patina decoration on a mirror

14

13

Stained glass

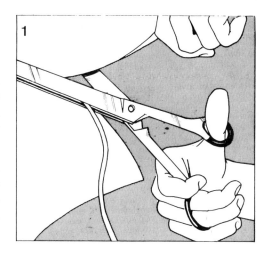

We could not end this book by passing over in silence this noble, secular art which is the ancestor of all painting on glass. This chapter will therefore cover the many aspects of preparing stained glass, and in particular grisaille, which is actually the only painting as such in the process.

Stained-glass windows are not only a coloured screen filtering light and letting only a part of it through, they are also barriers to keep the weather out. For that reason they have to be sturdy as well as decorative. Stained-glass technique has actually evolved very little since its beginnings. But it may surprise you to see in this chapter just how many operations go into making a window. One has to bring the highest craft and patience to bear on the task.

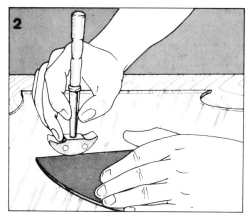

Sketch plan

This will organise the arrangement of the bits of glass which are to make up the window. It cannot reproduce the transparency of the finished work, but must take account of how the sun will shine through it, its architectural framework, the place it will stand in, its climate, the possibilities of materials used and a hundred other factors. The plan may be fifth, twelfth or twentieth scale, depending on the size of the window.

Colouring

This is the prime process in the whole operation. It is very chancy, and most often rests on the craftsman's experience alone. Optical glass is often very rich in textures created by irregularities. It is favoured by just this quality, governed by three important factors:

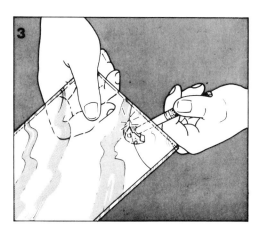

—variations in intensity of colour or shade caused by unequal thickness or pigment distribution, created a differentiated reflection.

—distribution of gas bubbles throughout the thickness of the glass, which are also important decorative elements.

—light stresses produced during blowing.

The colours must be determined by reference to the sketch.

Transferring the design

This must be done on strong paper, and include the inner and outer contours of the aperture, the outlines of the mullions and any other separating and strengthening elements and fixings, without forgetting the inner and outer outlines of the pieces of glass bordering each pane, the indications of grisaille or shading and the reference for each colour. Provide some vertical leadings in the bottom of each window to take the weight of the pane.

A precise tracing of the whole assembly should be made for calibrating the pieces of glass, for which the design should be reproduced on another sheet (150g).

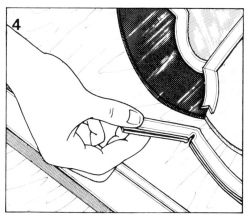

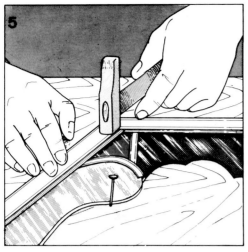

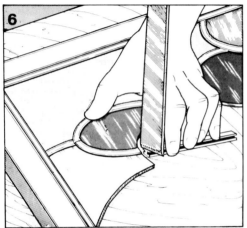

Cutting

Begin by cutting out this sheet into the outlines of the various pieces of glass. In the case of a straight-line break, do the cutting 1mm from the axis of the leading. For twisting curves three-bladed scissors are used, which will let you cut a fine strip 2mm thick (1). The actual cutting-out is done with a diamond cutter. Lean your left hand firmly on the template covering the glass and draw the counterturning tool towards you (2). The piece is separated by a rocking motion of the hand. When the size of the glass will not allow this, grasp it with pliers. For concave cuts, a few light well-placed blows with the diamond hammer are usually enough (3). Templates are especially useful in designs made up of repeated motifs.

Assembly

Once cut the pieces of glass and their templates are put in place on the sketch. They are then set in place with H-section lead strips. These will then be soldered together. This is done on a work-surface into which nails can be hammered as temporary stops (5) during assembly. Begin the setting by fixing the two lead pieces forming the left corner, and placing the corner piece in position. For sharp changes of direction nick the lead slightly (4) before bending it. Cut off the excess lead to fit the rims of the pieces with a sharp knife (6), having shaped any necessary curves by hand. The assembly must be as tight and solid as possible. When all the pieces are in place the other surrounding leads are fixed in place with pieces of wood. The lead is then pressed down onto the glass and encased round the edges.

Soldering

This is done with a soldering iron neither too hot nor too cold. You must first rub a little stearine flux (tallow is often used) over the edges in such a way that both lead and tin are scoured clean at the moment of soldering (9). Do not forget to rub the iron with a metal brush before tinning it. The soldered joint where the leads meet must be perfect right through to the centre, because an inadequate overlap will not give enough purchase to the solder. The other side of the stained-glass is then soldered, after the lead has been tapped down and stearine smeared on.

Mastic

You should waterproof the window with a clean paste made of whiting, linseed oil and fixative.

Painting the glass surfaces

This is to complete the design the lead makes up, to add details too fine to be outlined in lead, to set off the glass, or to change its colour by adding an extra tint. It is done by assembling the pieces of glass on a light table and immobilizing them with a spot of wax.

Grisaille should be put on in one layer only, because the glass is not absorbent. Grisaille paints must almost always be crushed with a palette knife and flat-bottomed pestle and mixed with a

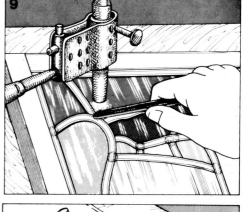

Stained-glass panes enhanced with grisaille lines

thinner and an adhesive. A dark red ochre grisaille, thinned with wine vinegar and adhering with gum arabic, will be needed for thin opaque lines; it should be put on with a fairly thick brush. Black and half-tones are obtained with water-based grisailles. The badger brush (10) will let you draw out soft tints by successive strokes made as smoothly as possible. The sable is also useful for texture work. The slightly moistened brush is dabbed vertically down onto the glass. It allows prepared shadings to be kept at the moment of application. Highlights and shadings are managed by taking away paint once the grisaille is completely dry. Lights and values can be touched up at the same time. Grisaille brings an added flexibility to stained-glass, and gives it a great wealth of effects and textures. It must, though, be fired on at 620°C.

1

2

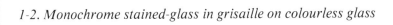

3

1-2. Monochrome stained-glass in grisaille on colourless glass

3. Restoration of a window showing the use of silver stain (silver sulphate)